Tower Air Fryer
Cookbook UK 2023

Crispy, Easy to Fry, Bake, Grill Recipes for Your Tower Air Fryer

Sofia Dawson

CONTENTS

INTRODUCTION

The air fryer is the latest kitchen appliance to sweep America off its feet. The air fryer promises to offer a healthy alternative to the very popular but deeply unhealthy fried food. Most people do not fry at home – with the exception of fried turkey at Thanksgiving – but nevertheless, the air fryer still offers great versatility. By cooking its food at very high temperatures almost immediately, it saves cooks a good deal of time and makes cooking a snap. Let's learn about the air fryer.

How Air Fryers Work

An air fryer cooks food by circulating hot air around the food through a traditional convection mechanism. The technology behind the air fryer is nothing exceptionally new. It uses the same process as a convection oven. The hot air is created by a very high-speed fan, which allows for a crispy top layer and tender, juicy interiors. The original air fryer was patented by Turbochef Technologies back in 2005, but its audience was hotel chains and other restaurants.

Phillips introduced its version of the air fryer in 2010 and marketed it to home chefs. The air fryer typically includes a round or egg-shaped fry basket that is easy to clean. Most of the fryer baskets are even dishwasher safe.

Is the Air Fryer Really Healthier?

According to Phillips, "the air fryer technology results in French fries that includes up to 80% less fat than traditionally-fried foods." But are these kinds of claims really true? According to studies, the answer is a qualified yes.

Deep fryers use about 50 times as much oil as their air frying counterparts. The electric fryer's main health benefit is that it cuts down on the amount of oil absorbed by the food, limiting the overall fat content. Food that is fried in oil is always unhealthy and has a lot of fat calories. A chicken breast that is fried has about 30 percent more fat than roasted chicken. An air fryer will not necessarily cook chicken healthier than baking it in an oven, but it will produce the crispy skin that people love in fried chicken.

Another benefit of an air fryer is avoiding the bad compounds which develop during the oil frying process. One of the compounds, acrylamide, may be linked to several cancers, including pancreatic, breast and ovarian cancer. The compound is created during high-heat cooking with oil. This compound does not form during the air frying process.

A study of the characteristics of French fries produced by deep fat frying and air frying found that the air fryer potatoes tasted like traditional French fries but with a substantially lower level of fat absorbed in the product. Again, this is due to the small amount of oil used in the air fryer.

However, you should not cook all of your foods in an air fryer, since air fryers still fry food. Fried foods are linked to heart conditions, high blood pressure, diabetes and some cancers. Limiting fried foods and focusing on healthy cooking methods such as roasting, steaming and sauteing are still best for daily cooking.

Beef, Pork & Lamb Recipes

Family Pork Loin Roast

Servings: 6   **Cooking Time: 55 minutes**

Ingredients:

- 1 ½ pounds boneless pork loin roast, washed
- 1 teaspoon mustard seeds
- 1 teaspoon garlic powder
- 1 teaspoon porcini powder
- 1 teaspoon shallot powder
- 3/4 teaspoon sea salt flakes
- 1 teaspoon red pepper flakes, crushed
- 2 dried sprigs thyme, crushed
- 2 tablespoons lime juice

Directions:

1. Firstly, score the meat using a small knife; make sure to not cut too deep.
2. In a small-sized mixing dish, combine all seasonings in the order listed above; mix to combine well.
3. Massage the spice mix into the pork meat to evenly distribute. Drizzle with lemon juice.
4. Then, set your Air Fryer to cook at 360 degrees F. Place the pork in the Air Fryer basket; roast for 25 to 30 minutes. Pause the machine, check for doneness and cook for 25 minutes more.

Italian Sausage Meatballs

👪 Servings: 8   🕐 Cooking Time: 15 minutes

Ingredients:

- 1 lb Italian sausage
- 1 lb ground beef
- 1/2 tsp Italian seasoning
- 1/2 tsp red pepper flakes
- 1 1/2 cups parmesan cheese, grated
- 2 egg, lightly beaten
- 2 tbsp parsley, chopped
- 2 garlic cloves, minced
- 1/4 cup onion, minced
- Pepper
- Salt

Directions:

1. Add all ingredients into the large mixing bowl and mix until well combined.
2. Spray air fryer basket with cooking spray.
3. Make meatballs from bowl mixture and place into the air fryer basket.
4. Cook at 350 F for 15 minutes.
5. Serve and enjoy.

Pork with Mushrooms

 Servings: 4   Cooking Time: 18 minutes

Ingredients:

- 1 lb pork chops, rinsed and pat dry
- 1/2 tsp garlic powder
- 1 tsp soy sauce
- 2 tbsp butter, melted
- 8 oz mushrooms, halved
- Pepper
- Salt

Directions:

1. Preheat the air fryer to 400 F.
2. Cut pork chops into the 3/4-inch cubes and place in a large mixing bowl.
3. Add remaining ingredients into the bowl and toss well.
4. Transfer pork and mushroom mixture into the air fryer basket and cook for 15-18 minutes. Shake basket halfway through.
5. Serve and enjoy.

Mini Beef Sausage Rolls

Servings: 4   Cooking Time: 35 minutes

Ingredients:

- 1 green onion, thinly sliced
- 8 mini puff pastry squares
- 1 cup flour
- 1 egg, beaten
- Salt and black pepper to taste

Directions:

1. Preheat the Air fryer to 360 F. Grease the air fryer basket with cooking spray.
2. In a bowl, mix beef sausage meat with green onion. Put the pastry squares on a floured surface. Divide the sausage mixture in the center of the pastry squares. Brush the edges with egg. Fold the squares and seal them. Transfer to the air fryer basket and brush the top of the rolls with the remaining egg. Cook for 20 minutes, flipping once halfway through until crisp and golden. Serve.

Garlic Pork Medallions

Servings: 4   **Cooking Time: 50 minutes**

Ingredients:

- 1-pound pork loin
- 2 tablespoons apple cider vinegar
- 2 tablespoons lemon juice
- ¼ cup heavy cream
- 1 teaspoon salt
- 1 teaspoon white pepper
- 1 garlic clove, diced
- 3 spring onions, diced
- 1 teaspoon lemon zest, grated
- 2 tablespoons avocado oil

Directions:

1. Make the marinade: in the mixing bowl mix up apple cider vinegar, lemon juice, heavy cream, salt, white pepper, diced garlic, onion, and lemon zest. Then add avocado oil and whisk the marinade carefully. Chop the pork loin roughly and put in the marinade. Coat the meat in the marinade carefully (use the spoon for this) and leave it for 20 minutes in the fridge. Meanwhile, preheat the air fryer to 365F. Put the marinated meat in the air fryer and cook it for 50 minutes. Stir the meat during cooking to avoid burning.

Saucy Lemony Beef Steaks

👪 Servings: 2   🕐 Cooking Time: 25 minutes

Ingredients:

- 1 pound beef steaks
- 4 tablespoons white wine
- 2 teaspoons crushed coriander seeds
- ½ teaspoon fennel seeds
- 1/3 cup beef broth
- 2 tablespoons lemon zest, grated
- 2 tablespoons canola oil
- 1/2 lemon, cut into wedges
- Salt flakes and freshly ground black pepper, to taste

Directions:

1. Heat the oil in a saucepan over a moderate flame. Then, cook the garlic for 1 minute, or until just fragrant.
2. Remove the pan from the heat; add the beef broth, wine, lemon zest, coriander seeds, fennel, salt flakes, and freshly ground black. Pour the mixture into a baking dish.
3. Add beef steaks to the baking dish; toss to coat well. Now, tuck the lemon wedges among the beef steaks.
4. Bake for 18 minutes at 335 degrees F. Serve warm.

Shallot and Celery Steak

👨‍👩‍👧 Servings: 6   🕐 Cooking Time: 17 minutes

Ingredients:

- 1/3 cup cream of shallot soup
- 2 sprigs fresh rosemary, chopped
- 1 cup celery, sliced
- 1/2 cup tomatoes, crushed
- 2 sprigs fresh thyme, chopped
- 1 teaspoon kosher salt
- 4 tablespoons dry white wine
- 1 teaspoon ground black pepper, or to taste
- 6 lean steaks, cut into strips
- 3 shallots, peeled and cut into wedges
- 1/2 teaspoon cayenne pepper

Directions:

1. Add all ingredients to an Air Fryer baking tray; then, cook for 13 minutes at 395 degrees F.

2. Work in batches; pause the machine once or twice to shake your food. Bon appétit!

Smoky Beef Burgers

👥 Servings: 4　🕐 Cooking Time: 10 minutes

Ingredients:

- 1 pound ground beef
- 4 whole-wheat hamburger buns, split and toasted
- 1 tablespoon Worcestershire sauce
- 1 teaspoon Maggi seasoning sauceo
- 3-4 drops liquid smoke
- 1 teaspoon dried parsley
- ½ teaspoon garlic powder
- ½ teaspoon onion powder
- Salt and ground black pepper, as required

Directions:

1. Preheat the Air fryer to 350 o F and grease an Air fryer basket.
2. Mix the beef, sauces, liquid smoke, parsley, and spices in a bowl.
3. Make 4 equal-sized patties from the beef mixture and arrange in the Air fryer basket.
4. Cook for about 10 minutes and dish out to serve on a bun.

Spicy Paprika Steak

Servings: 2   **Cooking Time: 20 minutes**

Ingredients:

- 1/2 Ancho chili pepper, soaked in hot water before using
- 1 tablespoon brandy
- 2 teaspoons smoked paprika
- 1 1/2 tablespoons olive oil
- 2 beef steaks
- Kosher salt, to taste
- 1 teaspoon ground allspice
- 3 cloves garlic, sliced

Directions:

1. Sprinkle the beef steaks with salt, paprika, and allspice. Add the steak to a baking dish that fits your fryer. Scatter the sliced garlic over the top.
2. Now, drizzle it with brandy and olive oil; spread minced Ancho chili pepper over the top.
3. Bake at 385 degrees F for 14 minutes, turning halfway through. Serve warm.

Sweet and Hot Ribs

Servings: 2   **Cooking Time: 30 minutes**

Ingredients:

- 1 tsp soy sauce
- Salt and pepper to season
- 1 tsp oregano
- 1 tbsp + 1 tbsp maple syrup
- 3 tbsp reduced sugar barbecue sauce
- 2 cloves garlic, minced
- 1 tbsp cayenne pepper
- 1 tsp sesame oil

Directions:

1. Put the chops on a chopping board and use a knife to cut them into smaller pieces of desired sizes. Put them in a mixing bowl, add the soy sauce, salt, pepper, oregano, one tablespoon of maple syrup, barbecue sauce, garlic, cayenne pepper, and sesame oil. Mix well and place the pork in the fridge to marinate in the spices for 5 hours.

2. Preheat the air fryer to 350 F. Open the air fryer and place the ribs in the fryer basket. Slide the fryer basket in and cook for 15 minutes. Open the air fryer, turn the ribs using tongs, apply the remaining maple syrup with a brush, close the air fryer, and continue cooking for 10 minutes.

Tangy Pork Roast

Servings: 8   **Cooking Time: 30 minutes**

Ingredients:

- 1 ½ tsp garlic powder
- 1 ½ tsp coriander powder
- ⅓ tsp salt
- 1 ½ tsp black pepper
- 1 ½ dried thyme
- 1 ½ tsp dried oregano
- 1 ½ tsp cumin powder
- 3 cups water
- 1 lemon, halved

Directions:

1. In a bowl, add garlic powder, coriander powder, salt, black pepper, thyme, oregano, and cumin powder. After the pork is well dried, poke holes all around it using a fork. Smear the oregano rub thoroughly on all sides with your hands and squeeze the lemon juice all over it. Leave to sit for 5 minutes.

2. Put the pork in the center of the fryer basket and cook for 10 minutes. Turn the pork with the help of two spatulas, increase the temperature to 350 F and continue cooking for 10 minutes.

3. Once ready, remove it and place it in on a chopping board to sit for 4 minutes before slicing. Serve the pork slices with a side of sautéed asparagus and hot sauce.

The Crispiest Roast Pork

 Servings: 4   Cooking Time: 10 minutes

Ingredients:

- 1 tsp five spice powder
- ½ tsp white pepper
- ¾ tsp garlic powder
- 1 tsp salt

Directions:

1. After blanching the pork belly, leave it cool at room temperature for 2 hours. Pat it dry with paper towels. Preheat the air fryer to 330 F. Take a skewer and pierce the skin as many times as you can, so you can ensure crispiness. Combine the seasonings in a small bowl, and rub it onto the pork.

2. Place the pork into the air fryer and cook for 30 minutes. Increase the temperature to 350 F and cook for 30 more minutes. Let cool slightly before serving.

Rosemary Beef Roast

Servings: 6   Cooking Time: 45 minutes

Ingredients:

- 2 lbs beef roast
- 1 tbsp olive oil
- 1 tsp rosemary
- 1 tsp thyme
- 1/4 tsp pepper
- 1 tsp salt

Directions:

1. Preheat the air fryer to 360 F.
2. Mix together oil, rosemary, thyme, pepper, and salt and rub over the meat.
3. Place meat in the air fryer and cook for 45 minutes.
4. Serve and enjoy.

Ribs and Chimichuri Mix

 Servings: 4   Cooking Time: 35 minutes

Ingredients:

- 1-pound pork baby back ribs, boneless
- 2 tablespoons chimichuri sauce
- ½ teaspoon salt

Directions:

1. Sprinkle the ribs with salt and brush with chimichuri sauce. Then preheat the air fryer to 365F. Put the pork ribs in the air fryer and cook for 35 minutes.

Tomato Riblets

 Servings: 4   Cooking Time: 40 minutes

Ingredients:

- 1-pound pork riblets
- 2 tablespoons Erythritol
- ½ teaspoon ground paprika
- ½ teaspoon chili powder
- 1 teaspoon yellow mustard
- 2 tablespoons apple cider vinegar
- 1 teaspoon keto tomato sauce
- ¼ cup of water
- 1 teaspoon salt

Directions:

1. In the mixing bowl mix up Erythritol, ground paprika, chili powder, yellow mustard, apple cider vinegar, tomato sauce, and water. Add salt. Whisk the mixture until homogenous. Then put the pork riblets in the homogenous mixture and mix up well. Leave the meat for 20 minutes in this sauce. After this, preheat the air fryer to 355F. Put the pork riblets in the air fryer and cook them for 40 minutes. Flip the pork ribs on another side after 20 minutes of cooking.

Lamb and Salsa

Servings: 4   **Cooking Time: 35 minutes**

Ingredients:

- 1 tablespoon chipotle powder
- A pinch of salt and black pepper
- 1 and ½ pounds lamb loin, cubed
- 2 tablespoons red vinegar
- 4 tablespoons olive oil
- 2 tomatoes, cubed
- 2 cucumbers, sliced
- 2 spring onions, chopped
- Juice of ½ lemon
- ¼ cup mint, chopped

Directions:

1. Heat up a pan that fits your air fryer with half of the oil over medium-high heat, add the lamb, stir and brown for 5 minutes. Add the chipotle powder, salt pepper and the vinegar, toss, put the pan in the air fryer and cook at 380 degrees F for 30 minutes. In a bowl, mix tomatoes with cucumbers, onions, lemon juice, mint and the rest of the oil and toss. Divide the lamb between plates, top each serving with the cucumber salsa and serve.

Delicious Burger

Servings: 2　　　**Cooking Time: 10 minutes**

Ingredients:

- 1/2 lb ground beef
- 1 tsp swerve
- 1 tsp ginger, minced
- 1/2 tbsp soy sauce
- 1 tbsp gochujang
- 1 tbsp green onion, chopped
- 1/2 tbsp sesame oil
- 1/4 tsp salt

Directions:

1. In a large bowl, mix together all ingredients until well combined. Place in refrigerator for 1 hour.
2. Make patties from beef mixture and place into the air fryer basket.
3. Cook at 360 F for 10 minutes.
4. Serve and enjoy.

Ultimate Ham Quiche Cups

👥 Servings: 18   🕐 Cooking Time: 25 minutes

Ingredients:

- 2 ¼ oz ham
- 1 cup milk
- ¼ tsp pepper
- 1 ½ cups swiss cheese, grated
- ¼ tsp salt
- ¼ cup green onion, chopped
- ½ tsp thyme

Directions:

1. Preheat your Fryer to 350 F. In a bowl, mix beaten eggs, thyme, onion, salt, Swiss cheese, pepper, and milk. Prepare baking forms and place ham slices in each baking form. Top with the egg mixture. Place the prepared muffin forms in your air fryer's cooking basket and cook for 15 minutes. Serve.

Very Tasty Herbed Burgers

Servings: 4   **Cooking Time: 25 minutes**

Ingredients:

- ¼ cup grated cheddar cheese
- ½ pound minced pork or beef
- 1 onion, chopped
- 1 tablespoon basil
- 1 teaspoon minced garlic
- 1 teaspoon mixed herbs
- 1 teaspoon mustard
- 1 teaspoon tomato puree
- 4 bread buns
- Mixed greens
- Salt and pepper to taste

Directions:

1. Preheat the air fryer to 3900F.
2. Place the grill pan accessory in the air fryer.
3. In a mixing bowl, combine the pork, onion, garlic, tomato puree, mustard, basil, mixed herbs, salt and pepper.
4. Form four patties using your hands.
5. Place on the grill pan accessory.
6. Cook for 25 minutes. Flip the burgers halfway through the cooking time.
7. Serve patties on bread buns and top with cheese and mixed greens.

Crisp Pork Chops

Servings: 6   **Cooking Time:** 12 minutes

Ingredients:

- 1 1/2 lbs pork chops, boneless
- 1 tsp paprika
- 1 tsp creole seasoning
- 1 tsp garlic powder
- 1/4 cup parmesan cheese, grated
- 1/3 cup almond flour

Directions:

1. Preheat the air fryer to 360 F.
2. Add all ingredients except pork chops in a zip-lock bag.
3. Add pork chops in the bag. Seal bag and shake well to coat pork chops.
4. Remove pork chops from zip-lock bag and place in the air fryer basket.
5. Cook pork chops for 10-12 minutes.
6. Serve and enjoy.

Vegetable & Side Dishes Recipes

Cranberry Beans Side Salad

Servings: 6   **Cooking Time: 15 minutes**

Ingredients:

- 6 garlic cloves, minced
- 2½ cups canned cranberry beans, drained
- 1 yellow onion, chopped
- 2 celery ribs, chopped
- ½ teaspoon smoked paprika
- ½ teaspoon red pepper flakes
- 3 teaspoons basil, chopped
- Salt and black pepper to taste
- 25 ounces canned tomatoes, drained and chopped
- 10 ounces kale, torn

Directions:

1. In a pan that fits your air fryer, add all of the ingredients and mix.
2. Place the pan in the fryer and cook at 370 degrees F for 15 minutes.
3. Divide between plates and serve as a side salad.

Healthy Green Beans

 Servings: 4   Cooking Time: 6 minutes

Ingredients:

- 1 lb green beans, trimmed
- Pepper
- Salt

Directions:

1. Spray air fryer basket with cooking spray.
2. Preheat the air fryer to 400 F.
3. Add green beans in air fryer basket and season with pepper and salt.
4. Cook green beans for 6 minutes. Turn halfway through.
5. Serve and enjoy.

Italian Eggplant Bites

 Servings: 5   Cooking Time: 10 minutes

Ingredients:

- 2 medium eggplants, trimmed
- 1 tomato
- 1 teaspoon Italian seasonings
- 1 teaspoon avocado oil
- 3 oz Parmesan, sliced

Directions:

1. Slice the eggplants on 5 slices. Then thinly slice the tomato on 5 slices. Place the eggplants in the air fryer in one layer and cook for 3 minutes from every side at 400F. After this, top the sliced eggplants with tomato, sprinkle with avocado oil and Italian seasonings. Then top the eggplants with Parmesan. Cook the meal for 4 minutes at 400F.

Gluten-Free Beans

 Servings: 2 🕐 Cooking Time: 10 minutes

Ingredients:

- 8 oz green beans, cut ends and cut beans in half
- 1 tsp sesame oil
- 1 tbsp tamari

Directions:

1. Add all ingredients into the zip-lock bag and shake well.
2. Place green beans into the air fryer basket and cook at 400 F for 10 minutes. Turn halfway through.
3. Serve and enjoy.

Garlic Radishes

🕐 Servings: 4 🕐 Cooking Time: 15 minutes

Ingredients:

- 20 radishes, halved
- 1 teaspoon chives, chopped
- 1 tablespoon garlic, minced
- Salt and black pepper to the taste
- 2 tablespoons olive oil

Directions:

1. In your air fryer's pan, combine all the ingredients and toss. Introduce the pan in the machine and cook at 370 degrees F for 15 minutes. Divide between plates and serve as a side dish.

Cumin Tofu

👥 Servings: 3   🕐 Cooking Time: 7 minutes

Ingredients:

- 1 cup tofu, cubed
- 1 tablespoon lime juice
- 2 tablespoons avocado oil
- ¼ teaspoon ground coriander
- ¼ teaspoon ground cumin
- ¼ teaspoon chili flakes

Directions:

1. In the mixing bowl mix up lime juice, avocado oil, ground coriander, cumin, and chili flakes. Then coat the tofu in the lime juice mixture well. Preheat the air fryer to 400F. Put the tofu cubes and all the oily liquid in the air fryer. Cook the tofu for 5 minutes. Then shake it well and cook for 2 minutes more.

Crispy Kale Chips

👥 Servings: 4   🕐 Cooking Time: 25 minutes

Ingredients:

- 2 tbsp olive oil
- 1 tsp garlic powder
- ½ tsp salt
- ¼ tsp onion powder
- ¼ tsp black pepper

Directions:

1. In a bowl, mix kale and oil together. Add in garlic, salt, onion, and pepper and toss to coate. Arrange the kale leaves on air fryer. Cook for 8 minutes at 350 F, shaking once. Leave to cool before serving.

Coconut Broccoli

👪 Servings: 4　　🕐 Cooking Time: 30 minutes

Ingredients:

- 3 tablespoons ghee, melted
- 15 ounces coconut cream
- 2 eggs, whisked
- 2 cups cheddar, grated
- 1 cup parmesan, grated
- 1 tablespoon mustard
- 1 pound broccoli florets
- A pinch of salt and black pepper
- 1 tablespoon parsley, chopped

Directions:

1. Grease a baking pan that fits the air fryer with the ghee and arrange the broccoli on the bottom. Add the cream, mustard, salt, pepper and the eggs and toss. Sprinkle the cheese on top, put the pan in the air fryer and cook at 380 degrees F for 30 minutes. Divide between plates and serve.

Cheesy Spinach

 Servings: 4   Cooking Time: 10 minutes

Ingredients:

- 14 ounces spinach
- 1 tablespoon olive oil
- 2 eggs, whisked
- 2 tablespoons milk
- 3 ounces cottage cheese
- Salt and black pepper to taste
- 1 yellow onion, chopped

Directions:

1. In a pan that fits your air fryer, heat up the oil over medium heat, add the onions, stir, and sauté for 2 minutes.
2. Add all other ingredients and toss.
3. Place the pan in the air fryer and cook at 380 degrees F for 8 minutes.
4. Divide the spinach between plates and serve as a side dish.

Cheesy Bacon Fries

Servings: 4   Cooking Time: 25 minutes

Ingredients:

- 5 slices bacon, chopped
- 2 tbsp vegetable oil
- 2½ cups Cheddar cheese, shredded
- 3 oz melted cream cheese
- Salt and pepper to taste
- ¼ cup scallions, chopped

Directions:

1. Preheat your air fryer to 400 F.
2. Add bacon to air fryer's basket and cook for 4, shaking once; set aside. Add in potatoes and drizzle oil on top to coat. Cook for 25 minutes, shaking the basket every 5 minutes. Season with salt and pepper.
3. In a bowl, mix cheddar cheese and cream cheese. Pour over the potatoes and cook for 5 more minutes at 340 F. Sprinkle chopped scallions on top and serve.

Butter Risotto

 Servings: 6   Cooking Time: 20 minutes

Ingredients:

- 2 tablespoons butter, melted
- 1 pound cauliflower, riced
- 2 garlic cloves, minced
- ½ cup chicken stock
- 1 cup heavy cream
- 1 cup parmesan, grated
- 3 tablespoons sun-dried tomatoes
- ½ teaspoon nutmeg, ground

Directions:

1. Heat up a pan that fits your air fryer with the butter over medium heat, add cauliflower rice, stir and cook for 2 minutes. Add the rest of the ingredients, toss, introduce the pan in the fryer and cook at 360 degrees F for 20 minutes. Divide between plates and serve as a side dish.

Dill Tomato

Servings: 2   Cooking Time: 8 minutes

Ingredients:

- 1 oz Parmesan, sliced
- 1 tomato
- 1 teaspoon fresh dill, chopped
- 1 teaspoon olive oil
- ¼ teaspoon dried thyme

Directions:

1. Trim the tomato and slice it on 2 pieces. Then preheat the air fryer to 350F. Top the tomato slices with sliced Parmesan, chopped fresh dill, and thyme. Sprinkle the tomatoes with olive oil and put in the air fryer. Cook the meal for 8 minutes. Remove cooked tomato parm from the air fryer with the help of the spatula.

Breaded Mushrooms

 Servings: 4   Cooking Time: 55 minutes

Ingredients:

- 2 cups breadcrumbs
- 2 eggs, beaten
- Salt and pepper to taste
- 2 cups Parmigiano Reggiano cheese, grated

Directions:

1. Preheat air fryer to 360 F. Pour breadcrumbs in a bowl, add salt and pepper and mix well. Pour cheese in a separate bowl. Dip each mushroom in the eggs, then in the crumbs, and then in the cheese. Slide-out the fryer basket and add 6 to 10 mushrooms. Cook for 20 minutes. Serve with cheese dip.

Famous Fried Pickles

 Servings: 6   Cooking Time: 20 minutes

Ingredients:

- 1/3 cup milk
- 1 teaspoon garlic powder
- 2 medium-sized eggs
- 1 teaspoon fine sea salt
- 1/3 teaspoon chili powder
- 1/3 cup all-purpose flour
- 1/2 teaspoon shallot powder
- 2 jars sweet and sour pickle spears

Directions:

1. Pat the pickle spears dry with a kitchen towel. Then, take two mixing bowls.
2. Whisk the egg and milk in a bowl. In another bowl, combine all dry ingredients.
3. Firstly, dip the pickle spears into the dry mix; then coat each pickle with the egg/milk mixture; dredge them in the flour mixture again for additional coating.
4. Air fry battered pickles for 15 minutes at 385 degrees. Enjoy!

Balsamic Radishes

 Servings: 4   🕐 Cooking Time: 15 minutes

Ingredients:

- 2 bunches red radishes, halved
- 1 tablespoon olive oil
- 2 tablespoons balsamic vinegar
- 2 tablespoons parsley, chopped
- Salt and black pepper to the taste

Directions:

1. In a bowl, mix the radishes with the remaining ingredients except the parsley, toss and put them in your air fryer's basket. Cook at 400 degrees F for 15 minutes, divide between plates, sprinkle the parsley on top and serve as a side dish.

Almond Cabbage

🕐 Servings: 4   🕐 Cooking Time: 13 minutes

Ingredients:

- 10 oz white cabbage
- ½ cup chicken broth
- ½ teaspoon salt
- ½ teaspoon ground paprika
- 1 teaspoon almond butter
- 4 oz Mozzarella, sliced

Directions:

1. Preheat the air fryer to 400F. Then insert the air fryer pan in the air fryer basket. Cut the white cabbage on the small patties and sprinkle them with salt. Crackle the cabbage to get juice from it. Then place it in the air fryer pan and sprinkle with ground paprika. Add almond butter and chicken broth. After this, cook the cabbage for 3 minutes. Then shake it well and top with Mozzarella. Cook the side dish for 10 minutes at 375F.

Fried Creamy Cabbage

Servings: 4   **Cooking Time: 30 minutes**

Ingredients:

- 1 green cabbage head; chopped.
- 1 yellow onion; chopped.
- 4 bacon slices; chopped.
- 1 cup whipped cream
- 2 tbsp. cornstarch
- Salt and black pepper to the taste

Directions:

1. Put cabbage, bacon and onion in your air fryer.
2. In a bowl; mix cornstarch with cream, salt and pepper, stir and add over cabbage. Toss, cook at 400 °F, for 20 minutes; divide among plates and serve as a side dish.

Keto Buddha Bowl

Servings: 3   **Cooking Time: 20 minutes**

Ingredients:

- 1 (1-pound) head cauliflower, food-processed into rice-like particles
- 2 bell pepper, spiralized
- Coarse sea salt and ground black pepper, to taste
- 3 cups baby spinach
- 2 tablespoons champagne vinegar
- 4 tablespoons mayonnaise
- 1 teaspoon yellow mustard
- 4 tablespoons olive oil, divided
- 2 tablespoons cilantro leaves, chopped
- 2 tablespoons pine nuts

Directions:

1. Start by preheating the Air Fryer to 400 degrees F.
2. Place the cauliflower florets and bell peppers in the lightly greased Air Fryer basket. Season with salt and black pepper; cook for 12 minutes, tossing halfway through the cooking time.
3. Toss with the baby spinach. Add the champagne vinegar, mayonnaise, mustard, and olive oil. Garnish with fresh cilantro and pine nuts. Bon appétit!

Air-Fried Brussels Sprouts

👪 Servings: 2   🕐 Cooking Time: 15 minutes

Ingredients:

- 1 tbsp butter, melted
- Salt and black pepper to taste
- ¼ tsp cayenne pepper

Directions:

1. In a bowl, mix Brussels sprouts, butter, cayenne pepper, salt, and pepper. Place Brussels sprouts in air fryer basket. Cook for 10 minutes at 380 F. Serve with sautéed onion rings.

Low-Carb Pita Chips

👪 Servings: 1   🕐 Cooking Time: 15 minutes

Ingredients:

- 1 cup mozzarella cheese, shredded
- 1 egg
- ¼ cup blanched finely ground flour
- ½ oz. pork rinds, finely ground

Directions:

1. Melt the mozzarella in the microwave. Add the egg, flour, and pork rinds and combine together to form a smooth paste. Microwave the cheese again if it begins to set.
2. Put the dough between two sheets of parchment paper and use a rolling pin to flatten it out into a rectangle. The thickness is up to you. With a sharp knife, cut into the dough to form triangles. It may be necessary to complete this step-in multiple batches.
3. Place the chips in the fryer and cook for five minutes at 350°F. Turn them over and cook on the other side for another five minutes, or until the chips are golden and firm.
4. Allow the chips to cool and harden further. They can be stored in an airtight container.

Snacks & Appetizers Recipes

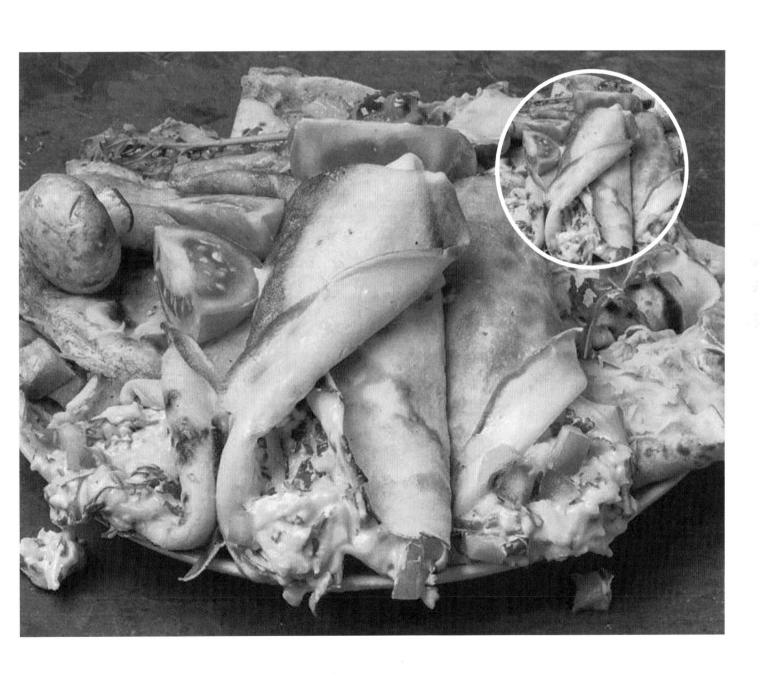

Paprika Potato Chips

 Servings: 3   🕐 Cooking Time: 50 minutes

Ingredients:

- 3 potatoes, thinly sliced
- 1 teaspoon sea salt
- 1 teaspoon garlic powder
- 1 teaspoon paprika
- 1/4 cup ketchup

Directions:

1. Add the sliced potatoes to a bowl with salted water. Let them soak for 30 minutes. Drain and rinse your potatoes.
2. Pat dry and toss with salt.
3. Cook in the preheated Air Fryer at 400 degrees F for 15 minutes, shaking the basket occasionally.
4. Work in batches. Toss with the garlic powder and paprika. Serve with ketchup. Enjoy!

Mini Pepper Poppers

Servings: 4   🕐 Cooking Time: 10 minutes

Ingredients:

- 8 mini sweet peppers
- ¼ cup pepper jack cheese, shredded
- 4 slices sugar-free bacon, cooked and crumbled
- 4 oz. full-fat cream cheese, softened

Directions:

1. Prepare the peppers by cutting off the tops and halving them lengthwise. Then take out the membrane and the seeds.
2. In a small bowl, combine the pepper jack cheese, bacon, and cream cheese, making sure to incorporate everything well
3. Spoon equal-sized portions of the cheese-bacon mixture into each of the pepper halves.
4. Place the peppers inside your fryer and cook for eight minutes at 400°F. Take care when removing them from the fryer and enjoy warm.

Pickled Bacon Bowls

 Servings: 4   🕒 Cooking Time: 20 minutes

Ingredients:

- 4 dill pickle spears, sliced in half and quartered
- 8 bacon slices, halved
- 1 cup avocado mayonnaise

Directions:

1. Wrap each pickle spear in a bacon slice, put them in your air fryer's basket and cook at 400 degrees F for 20 minutes. Divide into bowls and serve as a snack with the mayonnaise.

Italian Dip

🕒 Servings: 8   🕒 Cooking Time: 12 minutes

Ingredients:

- 8 oz cream cheese, softened
- 1 cup mozzarella cheese, shredded
- 1/2 cup roasted red peppers
- 1/3 cup basil pesto
- 1/4 cup parmesan cheese, grated

Directions:

1. Add parmesan cheese and cream cheese into the food processor and process until smooth.
2. Transfer cheese mixture into the air fryer pan and spread evenly.
3. Pour basil pesto on top of cheese layer.
4. Sprinkle roasted pepper on top of basil pesto layer.
5. Sprinkle mozzarella cheese on top of pepper layer and place dish in air fryer basket.
6. Cook dip at 250 F for 12 minutes.
7. Serve and enjoy.

Lemon Green Beans

Servings: 4   **Cooking Time: 20 minutes**

Ingredients:

- 1 lemon, juiced
- 1 lb. green beans, washed and destemmed
- ¼ tsp. extra virgin olive oil
- Sea salt to taste
- Black pepper to taste

Directions:

1. Pre-heat the Air Fryer to 400°F.
2. Put the green beans in your Air Fryer basket and drizzle the lemon juice over them.
3. Sprinkle on the pepper and salt. Pour in the oil, and toss to coat the green beans well.
4. Cook for 10 – 12 minutes and serve warm.
5. Pre-heat the Air Fryer to 400°F.
6. Put the green beans in your Air Fryer basket and drizzle the lemon juice over them.
7. Sprinkle on the pepper and salt. Pour in the oil, and toss to coat the green beans well.
8. Cook for 10 – 12 minutes and serve warm.

Cilantro Shrimp Balls

 Servings: 4   Cooking Time: 15 minutes

Ingredients:

- 1 pound shrimp, peeled, deveined and minced
- 1 egg, whisked
- 3 tablespoons coconut, shredded
- ½ cup coconut flour
- 1 tablespoon avocado oil
- 1 tablespoon cilantro, chopped

Directions:

1. In a bowl, mix all the ingredients, stir well and shape medium balls out of this mix Place the balls in your lined air fryer's basket, cook at 350 degrees F for 15 minutes and serve as an appetizer.

Chili Kale Chips

Servings: 4   Cooking Time: 5 minutes

Ingredients:

- 1 teaspoon nutritional yeast
- 1 teaspoon salt
- 2 cups kale, chopped
- ½ teaspoon chili flakes
- 1 teaspoon sesame oil

Directions:

1. Mix up kale leaves with nutritional yeast, salt, chili flakes, and sesame oil. Shake the greens well. Preheat the air fryer to 400F and put the kale leaves in the air fryer basket. Cook them for 3 minutes and then give a good shake. Cook the kale leaves for 2 minutes more.

Chicken and Berries Bowls

Servings: 2   **Cooking Time: 20 minutes**

Ingredients:

- 1 chicken breast, skinless, boneless and cut into strips
- 2 cups baby spinach
- 1 cup blueberries
- 6 strawberries, chopped
- ½ cup walnuts, chopped
- 3 tablespoons balsamic vinegar
- 1 tablespoon olive oil
- 3 tablespoons feta cheese, crumbled

Directions:

1. Heat up a pan that fits the air fryer with the oil over medium heat, add the meat and brown it for 5 minutes. Add the rest of the ingredients except the spinach, toss, introduce in the fryer and cook at 370 degrees F for 15 minutes. Add the spinach, toss, cook for another 5 minutes, divide into bowls and serve.

Cheesy Broccoli Balls

👥 Servings: 6   🕐 Cooking Time: 20 minutes

Ingredients:

- 2 eggs, well whisked
- 2 cups Colby cheese, shredded
- 1 cup flour
- Seasoned salt, to taste
- ¼ tsp. ground black pepper, or more if preferred
- 1 head broccoli, chopped into florets
- 1 cup crushed saltines

Directions:

1. Mix together the eggs, cheese, flour, salt, pepper, and broccoli until a dough-like paste is formed.
2. Refrigerate for 1 hour. Divide the mixture evenly and mold each portion into small balls. Coat the balls in the crushed saltines and spritz them all over with cooking spray.
3. Cook at 360°F for 10 minutes. At this point, you should check how far along in the cooking process they are and allow to cook for a further 8 - 10 minutes as needed.
4. Serve with the dipping sauce of your choice.

Cheese Dip

 Servings: 10   Cooking Time: 10 minutes

Ingredients:

- 1 pound mozzarella, shredded
- 1 tablespoon thyme, chopped
- 6 garlic cloves, minced
- 3 tablespoons olive oil
- 1 teaspoon rosemary, chopped
- A pinch of salt and black pepper

Directions:

1. In a pan that fits your air fryer, mix all the ingredients, whisk really well, introduce in the air fryer and cook at 370 degrees F for 10 minutes. Divide into bowls and serve right away.

Cauliflower Poppers

Servings: 6   Cooking Time: 16 minutes

Ingredients:

- 1 large head cauliflower, cut into bite-sized florets
- 2 tablespoons olive oil
- Salt and freshly ground black pepper, as needed

Directions:

1. Drizzle the cauliflower florets with oil.
2. Sprinkle with salt and black pepper.
3. Set the temperature of Air Fryer to 390 degrees F.
4. Place the cauliflower florets in a greased Air Fryer basket in a single layer in 2 batches.
5. Air Fry for about 8 minutes, shaking once halfway through.
6. Serve hot.

Broccoli Florets

 Servings: 4   🕐 Cooking Time: 20 minutes

Ingredients:

- 1 lb. broccoli, cut into florets
- 1 tbsp. lemon juice
- 1 tbsp. olive oil
- 1 tbsp. sesame seeds
- 3 garlic cloves, minced

Directions:

1. In a bowl, combine all of the ingredients, coating the broccoli well.
2. Transfer to the Air Fryer basket and air fry at 400°F for 13 minutes.

Cod Nuggets

🕐 Servings: 4   🕐 Cooking Time: 10 minutes

Ingredients:

- 1 cup all-purpose flour
- 2 eggs
- ¾ cup breadcrumbs
- 1 pound cod, cut into 1x2½-inch strips
- A pinch of salt
- 2 tablespoons olive oil

Directions:

1. Preheat the Air fryer to 390 o F and grease an Air fryer basket.
2. Place flour in a shallow dish and whisk the eggs in a second dish.
3. Place breadcrumbs, salt, and olive oil in a third shallow dish.
4. Coat the cod strips evenly in flour and dip in the eggs.
5. Roll into the breadcrumbs evenly and arrange the nuggets in an Air fryer basket.
6. Cook for about 10 minutes and dish out to serve warm.

Garlic Potatoes

Servings: 4   **Cooking Time: 40 minutes**

Ingredients:

- 1 lb. russet baking potatoes
- 1 tbsp. garlic powder
- 1 tbsp. freshly chopped parsley
- ½ tsp. salt
- ¼ tsp. black pepper
- 1 – 2 tbsp. olive oil

Directions:

1. Wash the potatoes and pat them dry with clean paper towels.
2. Pierce each potato several times with a fork.
3. Place the potatoes in a large bowl and season with the garlic powder, salt and pepper.
4. Pour over the olive oil and mix well.
5. Pre-heat the Air Fryer to 360°F.
6. Place the potatoes in the fryer and cook for about 30 minutes, shaking the basket a few times throughout the cooking time.
7. Garnish the potatoes with the chopped parsley and serve with butter, sour cream or another dipping sauce if desired.

Beans and Veggie Burgers

👫 Servings: 4   🕐 Cooking Time: 23 minutes

Ingredients:

- 1 cup cooked black beans
- 2 cups boiled potatoes, peeled and mashed
- 1 cup fresh spinach, chopped
- 1 cup fresh mushrooms, chopped
- 6 cups fresh baby greens
- 2 teaspoons Chile lime seasoning
- Olive oil cooking spray

Directions:

1. Preheat the Air fryer to 375 o F and grease an Air fryer basket.

2. Mix together potatoes, spinach, beans, mushrooms and Chile lime seasoning in a large bowl.

3. Make 4 equal-sized patties from this mixture and place the patties into the prepared Air fryer basket.

4. Spray with olive oil cooking spray and cook for about 20 minutes, flipping once in between.

5. Set the Air fryer to 90 o F and cook for about 3 more minutes.

6. Dish out in a platter and serve alongside the baby greens.

Fish & Seafood Recipes

Fishman Cakes

Servings: 4   **Cooking Time: 35 minutes**

Ingredients:

- 2 cups white fish
- 1 cup potatoes, mashed
- 1 tsp. mix herbs
- 1 tsp. mix spice
- 1 tsp. coriander
- 1 tsp. Worcestershire sauce
- 2 tsp. chili powder
- 1 tsp. milk
- 1 tsp. butter
- 1 small onion, diced
- ¼ cup bread crumbs
- Pepper and salt to taste

Directions:

1. Place all of the ingredients in a bowl and combine.
2. Using your hands, mold equal portions of the mixture into small patties and refrigerate for 2 hours.
3. Put the fish cakes in the Air Fryer basket and cook at 400°F for 15 minutes. Serve hot.

Garlicky Squid

Servings: 4 **Cooking Time: 25 minutes**

Ingredients:

- 1 pound squid, cleaned and cut into small pieces
- 10 garlic cloves, minced
- 1 teaspoon ginger piece, grated
- 2 green chilies, chopped
- 2 yellow onions, chopped
- ½ tablespoon lemon juice
- 1 tablespoon coriander powder
- ¾ tablespoon chili powder
- Salt and black pepper to taste
- 1 teaspoon mustard seeds, toasted
- ½ cup chicken stock
- 3 tablespoons olive oil

Directions:

1. Place all ingredients into a pan that fits your air fryer and toss.
2. Put the pan in the air fryer and cook at 380 degrees F for 25 minutes.
3. Divide between plates and serve.

Catfish Bites

Servings: 4   **Cooking Time: 10 minutes**

Ingredients:

- ¼ cup coconut flakes
- 3 tablespoons coconut flour
- 1 teaspoon salt
- 3 eggs, beaten
- 10 oz catfish fillet
- Cooking spray

Directions:

1. Cut the catfish fillet on the small pieces (nuggets) and sprinkle with salt. After this, dip the catfish pieces in the egg and coat in the coconut flour. Then dip the fish pieces in the egg again and coat in the coconut flakes. Preheat the air fryer to 385F.
2. Place the catfish nuggets in the air fryer basket and cook them for 6 minutes. Then flip the nuggets on another side and cook them for 4 minutes more.

Cajun Shrimps

Servings: 4   **Cooking Time: 6 minutes**

Ingredients:

- 8 oz shrimps, peeled
- 1 teaspoon Cajun spices
- 1 teaspoon cream cheese
- 1 egg, beaten
- ½ teaspoon salt
- 1 teaspoon avocado oil

Directions:

1. Sprinkle the shrimps with Cajun spices and salt. In the mixing bowl mix up cream cheese and egg, Dip every shrimp in the egg mixture. Preheat the air fryer to 400F.
2. Place the shrimps in the air fryer and sprinkle with avocado oil. Cook the popcorn shrimps for 6 minutes. Shake them well after 3 minutes of cooking.

Buttery Chives Trout

Servings: 4   **Cooking Time: 12 minutes**

Ingredients:

- 4 trout fillets, boneless
- 4 tablespoons butter, melted
- Salt and black pepper to the taste
- Juice of 1 lime
- 1 tablespoon chives, chopped
- 1 tablespoon parsley, chopped

Directions:

1. Mix the fish fillets with the melted butter, salt and pepper, rub gently, put the fish in your air fryer's basket and cook at 390 degrees F for 6 minutes on each side. Divide between plates and serve with lime juice drizzled on top and with parsley and chives sprinkled at the end.

Buttered Scallops

Servings: 2   **Cooking Time: 4 minutes**

Ingredients:

- ¾ pound sea scallops, cleaned and patted very dry
- 1 tablespoon butter, melted
- ½ tablespoon fresh thyme, minced
- Salt and black pepper, as required

Directions:

1. Preheat the Air fryer to 390 o F and grease an Air fryer basket.
2. Mix scallops, butter, thyme, salt, and black pepper in a bowl.
3. Arrange scallops in the Air fryer basket and cook for about 4 minutes.
4. Dish out the scallops in a platter and serve hot.

Creamy Tuna Cakes

Servings: 4　　**Cooking Time: 15 minutes**

Ingredients:

- 2 (6-ounces) cans tuna, drained
- 1½ tablespoon almond flour
- 1½ tablespoons mayonnaise
- 1 tablespoon fresh lemon juice
- 1 teaspoon dried dill
- 1 teaspoon garlic powder
- ½ teaspoon onion powder
- Pinch of salt and ground black pepper

Directions:

1. Preheat the Air fryer to 400 o F and grease an Air fryer basket.
2. Mix the tuna, mayonnaise, almond flour, lemon juice, dill, and spices in a large bowl.
3. Make 4 equal-sized patties from the mixture and arrange in the Air fryer basket.
4. Cook for about 10 minutes and flip the sides.
5. Cook for 5 more minutes and dish out the tuna cakes in serving plates to serve warm.

Butter Mussels

👪 Servings: 5　🕐 Cooking Time: 2 minutes

Ingredients:

- 2-pounds mussels
- 1 shallot, chopped
- 1 tablespoon minced garlic
- 1 tablespoon butter, melted
- 1 teaspoon sunflower oil
- 1 teaspoon salt
- 1 tablespoon fresh parsley, chopped
- ½ teaspoon chili flakes

Directions:

1. Clean and wash mussels and put them in the big bowl. Add shallot, minced garlic, butter, sunflower oil, salt, and chili flakes. Shake the mussels well. Preheat the air fryer to 390F. Put the mussels in the air fryer basket and cook for 2 minutes. Then transfer the cooked meal in the serving bowl and top it with chopped fresh parsley.

Great Cat Fish

👪 Servings: 4   🕐 Cooking Time: 25 minutes

Ingredients:

- ¼ cup seasoned fish fry
- 1 tbsp olive oil
- 1 tbsp parsley, chopped

Directions:

1. Preheat your air fryer to 400 F, and add seasoned fish fry, and fillets in a large Ziploc bag; massage well to coat. Place the fillets in your air fryer's cooking basket and cook for 10 minutes. Flip the fish and cook for 2-3 more minutes. Top with parsley and serve.

Breaded Hake

👪 Servings: 2   🕐 Cooking Time: 12 minutes

Ingredients:

- 1 egg
- 4 ounces breadcrumbs
- 4 (6-ounces) hake fillets
- 1 lemon, cut into wedges
- 2 tablespoons vegetable oil

Directions:

1. Preheat the Air fryer to 350 o F and grease an Air fryer basket.
2. Whisk the egg in a shallow bowl and mix breadcrumbs and oil in another bowl.
3. Dip hake fillets into the whisked egg and then, dredge in the breadcrumb mixture.
4. Arrange the hake fillets into the Air fryer basket in a single layer and cook for about 12 minutes.
5. Dish out the hake fillets onto serving plates and serve, garnished with lemon wedges.

Herbed Haddock

👥 Servings: 2   🕐 Cooking Time: 8 minutes

Ingredients:

- 2 (6-ounce) haddock fillets
- 2 tablespoons pine nuts
- 3 tablespoons fresh basil, chopped
- 1 tablespoon Parmesan cheese, grated
- ½ cup extra-virgin olive oil
- Salt and black pepper, to taste

Directions:

1. Preheat the Air fryer to 355 o F and grease an Air fryer basket.
2. Coat the haddock fillets evenly with olive oil and season with salt and black pepper.
3. Place the haddock fillets in the Air fryer basket and cook for about 8 minutes.
4. Dish out the haddock fillets in serving plates.
5. Meanwhile, put remaining ingredients in a food processor and pulse until smooth.
6. Top this cheese sauce over the haddock fillets and serve hot.

Baked Cod

Servings: 4   **Cooking Time: 12 minutes**

Ingredients:

- 4 cod fillets, boneless
- Salt and black pepper to taste
- 2 tablespoons parsley, chopped
- A drizzle of olive oil
- ¾ teaspoon sweet paprika
- ½ teaspoon oregano, dried
- ½ teaspoon thyme, dried
- ½ teaspoon basil, dried
- Juice of 1 lemon
- 2 tablespoons butter, melted

Directions:

1. Add all ingredients to a bowl and toss gently.
2. Transfer the fish to your air fryer and cook at 380 degrees F for 6 minutes on each side.
3. Serve right away.

Hot Crab Cakes

👥 Servings: 8   🕐 Cooking Time: 20 minutes

Ingredients:

- 2 eggs, beaten
- ½ cup breadcrumbs
- ⅓ cup finely chopped green onion
- ¼ cup parsley, chopped
- 1 tbsp mayonnaise
- 1 tsp sweet chili sauce
- ½ tsp paprika
- Salt and black pepper
- Cooking spray

Directions:

1. In a bowl, add meat, eggs, crumbs, green onion, parsley, mayo, chili sauce, paprika, salt, and pepper and mix well with hands. Shape into 8 cakes and grease them lightly with oil. Arrange the cakes into a fryer, without overcrowding. Cook for 8 minutes at 400 F, turning once halfway through cooking.

Air Fried Catfish

 Servings: 4   Cooking Time: 20 minutes

Ingredients:

- 4 catfish fillets
- 1 tbsp olive oil
- 1/4 cup fish seasoning
- 1 tbsp fresh parsley, chopped

Directions:

1. Preheat the air fryer to 400 F.
2. Spray air fryer basket with cooking spray.
3. Seasoned fish with seasoning and place into the air fryer basket.
4. Drizzle fish fillets with oil and cook for 10 minutes.
5. Turn fish to another side and cook for 10 minutes more.
6. Garnish with parsley and serve.

Jumbo Shrimp

 Servings: 4   Cooking Time: 10 minutes

Ingredients:

- 12 jumbo shrimps
- ½ tsp. garlic salt
- ¼ tsp. freshly cracked mixed peppercorns

For the Sauce:

- 1 tsp. Dijon mustard
- 4 tbsp. mayonnaise
- 1 tsp. lemon zest
- 1 tsp. chipotle powder
- ½ tsp. cumin powder

Directions:

1. Sprinkle the garlic salt over the shrimp and coat with the cracked peppercorns.
2. Fry the shrimp in the cooking basket at 395°F for 5 minutes.
3. Turn the shrimp over and allow to cook for a further 2 minutes.
4. In the meantime, mix together all ingredients for the sauce with a whisk.
5. Serve over the shrimp.

Desserts Recipes

Chocolate Cheesecake

Servings: 4   **Cooking Time:** 60 minutes

Ingredients:

- 4 oz cream cheese
- ½ oz heavy cream
- 1 tsp Sugar Glycerite
- 1 tsp Splenda
- 1 oz Enjoy Life mini chocolate chips

Directions:

1. Combine all the ingredients except the chocolate to a thick consistency.
2. Fold in the chocolate chips.
3. Refrigerate in serving cups.
4. Serve!

Chocolate Lover's Muffins

🛉 Servings: 8   🕐 Cooking Time: 10 minutes

Ingredients:

- 1½ cups all-purpose flour
- 2 teaspoons baking powder
- 1 egg
- 1 cup yogurt
- ½ cup mini chocolate chips
- ¼ cup sugar
- Salt, to taste
- 1/3 cup vegetable oil
- 2 teaspoons vanilla extract

Directions:

1. Preheat the Air fryer to 355 o F and grease 8 muffin cups lightly.
2. Mix flour, baking powder, sugar and salt in a bowl.
3. Whisk egg, oil, yogurt and vanilla extract in another bowl.
4. Combine the flour and egg mixtures and mix until a smooth mixture is formed.
5. Fold in the chocolate chips and divide this mixture into the prepared muffin cups.
6. Transfer into the Air fryer basket and cook for about 10 minutes.
7. Refrigerate for 2 hours and serve chilled.

Chocolate Balls

Servings: 8   **Cooking Time: 13 minutes**

Ingredients:

- 2 cups plain flour
- 2 tablespoons cocoa powder
- ¾ cup chilled butter
- ¼ cup chocolate, chopped into 8 chunks
- ½ cup icing sugar
- Pinch of ground cinnamon
- 1 teaspoon vanilla extract

Directions:

1. Preheat the Air fryer to 355 o F and grease a baking dish lightly.
2. Mix flour, icing sugar, cocoa powder, cinnamon and vanilla extract in a bowl.
3. Add cold butter and buttermilk and mix until a smooth dough is formed.
4. Divide the dough into 8 equal balls and press 1 chocolate chunk in the center of each ball.
5. Cover completely with the dough and arrange the balls in a baking dish.
6. Transfer into the Air fryer and cook for about 8 minutes.
7. Set the Air fryer to 320 o F and cook for 5 more minutes.
8. Dish out in a platter and serve to enjoy.

Bread Pudding

👥 Servings: 2   🕐 Cooking Time: 12 minutes

Ingredients:

- 1 cup milk
- 1 egg
- 2 tablespoons raisins, soaked in hot water for about 15 minutes
- 2 bread slices, cut into small cubes
- 1 tablespoon chocolate chips
- 1 tablespoon brown sugar
- ½ teaspoon ground cinnamon
- ¼ teaspoon vanilla extract
- 1 tablespoon sugar

Directions:

1. Preheat the Air fryer to 375 o F and grease a baking dish lightly.
2. Mix milk, egg, brown sugar, cinnamon and vanilla extract until well combined.
3. Stir in the raisins and mix well.
4. Arrange the bread cubes evenly in the baking dish and top with the milk mixture.
5. Refrigerate for about 20 minutes and sprinkle with chocolate chips and sugar.
6. Transfer the baking pan into the Air fryer and cook for about 12 minutes.
7. Dish out and serve immediately.

Cinnamon Fried Plums

Servings: 6　　**Cooking Time: 20 minutes**

Ingredients:

- 6 plums, cut into wedges
- 1 teaspoon ginger, ground
- ½ teaspoon cinnamon powder
- Zest of 1 lemon, grated
- 2 tablespoons water
- 10 drops stevia

Directions:

1. In a pan that fits the air fryer, combine the plums with the rest of the ingredients, toss gently, put the pan in the air fryer and cook at 360 degrees F for 20 minutes. Serve cold.

Delicious Spiced Apples

Servings: 6　　**Cooking Time: 10 minutes**

Ingredients:

- 4 small apples, sliced
- 1 tsp apple pie spice
- 1/2 cup erythritol
- 2 tbsp coconut oil, melted

Directions:

1. Add apple slices in a mixing bowl and sprinkle sweetener, apple pie spice, and coconut oil over apple and toss to coat.
2. Transfer apple slices in air fryer dish. Place dish in air fryer basket and cook at 350 F for 10 minutes.
3. Serve and enjoy.

Baked Apples

Servings: 2   Cooking Time: 35 minutes

Ingredients:

- 2 tbsp butter, cold
- 3 tbsp sugar
- 3 tbsp crushed walnuts
- 2 tbsp raisins
- 1 tsp cinnamon

Directions:

1. Preheat the Air fryer to 400 F.
2. In a bowl, add butter, sugar, walnuts, raisins and cinnamon; mix with fingers until you obtain a crumble. Arrange the apples in the air fryer. Stuff the apples with the filling mixture. Cook for 30 minutes.

Egg Custard

Servings: 6   Cooking Time: 32 minutes

Ingredients:

- 2 egg yolks
- 3 eggs
- 1/2 cup erythritol
- 2 cups heavy whipping cream
- 1/2 tsp vanilla
- 1 tsp nutmeg

Directions:

1. Preheat the air fryer to 325 F.
2. Add all ingredients into the large bowl and beat until well combined.
3. Pour custard mixture into the greased baking dish and place into the air fryer.
4. Cook for 32 minutes.
5. Let it cool completely then place in the refrigerator for 1-2 hours.
6. Serve and enjoy.

Bacon Cookies

Servings: 2   **Cooking Time: 15 minutes**

Ingredients:

- ¼ tsp. ginger
- 1/5 tsp. baking soda
- 2/3 cup peanut butter
- 2 tbsp. Swerve
- 3 slices bacon, cooked and chopped

Directions:

1. In a bowl, mix the ginger, baking soda, peanut butter, and Swerve together, making sure to combine everything well.
2. Stir in the chopped bacon.
3. With clean hands, shape the mixture into a cylinder and cut in six. Press down each slice into a cookie with your palm.
4. Pre-heat your fryer at 350°F.
5. When the fryer is warm, put the cookies inside and cook for seven minutes. Take care when taking them out of the fryer and allow to cool before serving.

Flavorsome Peach Cake

Servings: 6   **Cooking Time: 40 minutes**

Ingredients:

- 1/2 pound peaches, pitted and mashed
- 3 tablespoons honey
- 1/2 teaspoon baking powder
- 1 ¼ cups cake flour
- 1/2 teaspoon orange extract
- 1 teaspoon pure vanilla extract
- 1/4 teaspoon ground cinnamon
- 1/3 cup ghee
- 1/8 teaspoon salt
- 1/2 cup caster sugar
- 2 eggs
- 1/4 teaspoon freshly grated nutmeg

Directions:

1. Firstly, preheat the air fryer to 310 degrees F. Spritz the cake pan with a nonstick cooking spray.
2. In a mixing bowl, beat the ghee with caster sugar until creamy. Fold in the egg, mashed peaches and honey.
3. Then, make the cake batter by mixing the remaining ingredients; now, stir in the peach/honey mixture.
4. Now, transfer the prepared batter to the cake pan; level the surface with a spoon.
5. Bake for 35 minutes or until a tester inserted in the center of your cake comes out completely dry. Enjoy!

Printed in Great Britain
by Amazon

87735059R00041